A Welsh Mining Village

Stuart Broomfield

Photographs by Chris Fairclough

Adam & Charles Black · London

The Silverthorne family live in a small terraced house in the village of Six Bells. Aneurin Silverthorne (Nye to his friends) is a miner; his wife Anne works in the corner shop. Amanda, aged eleven, and Adrian, aged ten, both go to the local junior school.

If you look at the map, you will see that Six Bells is in the county of Gwent in South Wales. It is part of the larger town of Abertillery, but the people who live in Six Bells always say they come from the village and not from the town.

Broomfield, Stuart
    A Welsh mining village. – (The 'Strands' series; 10).
    1. Six Bells, Wales – Social life and customs –
Juvenile literature
    2. Wales – Social life and customs – Juvenile
literature
    I. Title   II. Fairclough, Chris   III. Series
    942.9'95   DA745.S/

    ISBN 0-7136-2084-6

Acknowledgements

The publishers would like to thank the following for permission to
reproduce photographs: Abertillery Museum Society pp. 4, 5, 6; Radio
Times Hulton Picture Library p. 19.
The map is by Frances Mackay
The artwork is by John Shackell

Published by A & C Black (Publishers) Limited
35 Bedford Row, London WC1R 4JH
ISBN 0 7136 2084 6

First published in 1981
© 1981 Stuart Broomfield and Chris Fairclough

Filmset and printed in Great Britain by
BAS Printers Limited, Over Wallop, Hampshire

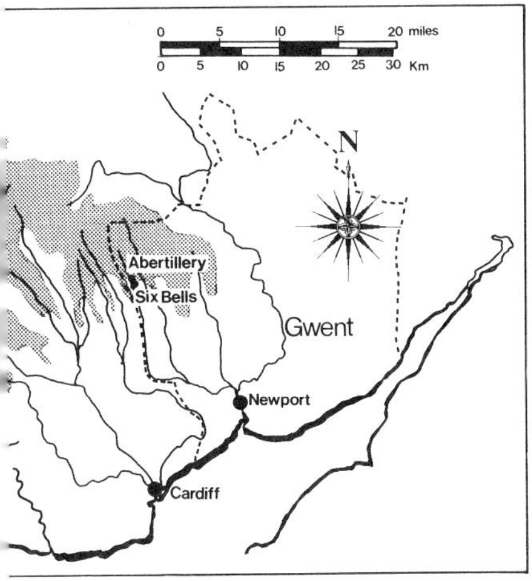

Six Bells is a mining village. It was built because coal was found in the valley. Nearly all the houses are in the bottom of the valley, close to the pit. The sides of the valley are very steep.

Gwent

Abertillery

Six Bells

Newport

Cardiff

N

Six Bells

The men who sank Six Bells pit in 1889

The colliery was opened in 1889. Before that, hardly anyone lived in the area. There were only a few farms. During the shooting season, parties of rich people came to shoot grouse on the hills.

When the colliery opened, men came with their families from England to work in it. They lived in terraced houses built by the company which owned the colliery. In those days, nearly everyone who lived in Six Bells worked at the pit.

Today, many people living in Six Bells have to find jobs in the larger towns nearby. The coal seams are thin, and it gets more and more difficult to dig the coal out. The colliery is not as big as it used to be; in and around the village you can see the ruins of the old colliery buildings.

During the 1920s and 30s, there was even less work for the miners, and it was much more difficult to get other jobs. Because they had nothing else to do, some of the unemployed miners decided to build a park. It is still there, and Adrian often plays football in it after school.

In the past, when nearly everybody lived and worked in Six Bells, there was a special feeling of togetherness. And today, something of this feeling still survives. Everybody knows each other, and most families have relatives living nearby. Adrian and Amanda's grandmother lives just a few streets away.

In a mining village, everyone is afraid of one thing—an accident at the pit. In 1960 there was a terrible disaster in Six Bells when there was a gas explosion underground. Nye still remembers that awful day.

Relatives and friends wait for news after the 1960 explosion

'It happened at 11.20 in the morning while I was still asleep. I'd been working on the night shift. As soon as I heard about it, I went down to the mine to help with the rescue. I can honestly say it was the worst experience I've ever had in my life.'

Dozens of men were trapped underground after the explosion. Relatives and friends waited anxiously at the pit head for news of the victims.

Forty-five men were killed. The whole village turned out to mourn them at their funeral.

Six Bells mourns the dead miners

Amanda and Adrian both go to Bryngwyn Junior School. Their father went to the same school when he was a boy. It's just a short walk from their house. When Amanda and Adrian are older, they will have to take the bus to the big comprehensive at the top of the valley.

Adrian likes games lessons best. 'I play football a lot. We play at school, at break-time and when we get home. I'm in the school five-a-side team. My favourite team is Manchester United. When I grow up I'd like to be a lorry driver so I can go to places like Manchester.'

When he's not playing football, Adrian rides his bicycle up and down the hilly streets. Sometimes he and his friends race each other down the side of the hill. From the top of the hill you can see the whole village spread out below.

Three nights a week Amanda goes to jazz band practice. Jazz bands are very popular in South Wales, and there is usually at least one in every village.

Nearly all band members play a 'gazoo'. This looks rather like a trumpet, and it is played by humming a tune through the mouthpiece. The 'gazooters' march behind the drummers, who are led by a drum majorette swirling a baton.

'Our band is called the RSMs, because we're trained by a man who used to be a Regimental Sergeant Major', Amanda explains. 'Our uniforms are the same as the Royal Welch Regiment, and we sometimes have discos to raise money to buy them. Nearly every weekend we go to other villages and towns to play in a competition.'

The Gwent RSMs have won many competitions. They were specially pleased to win one which was held recently on their home ground, Six Bells Park.

Getting to and from Six Bells can be quite a
problem. There are no passenger trains, and the
buses are very expensive. Years ago, there used to
be a regular rail service up and down the valley,
and just below the village there was an important
railway junction. Today the old railway lines are
only used by freight trains.

Nowadays, nearly every family in Six Bells has a car. Many people drive to one of the new large supermarkets to do their weekly shopping. But there are still several small shops in the village for everyday needs. Anne works in one of these, six afternoons a week. She does most of her shopping there too.

Anne is always busy. In the mornings there is housework to do, and in the afternoons she serves in the shop. When she gets back home, she has to make supper. The only time she can relax is in the evening, when she likes to watch television.

13

The mine is open twenty-four hours a day. The work is divided into three main shifts—the morning, afternoon, and night shift. Nye works on the night shift. He sets off for work at 9 o'clock at night and returns at 6 in the morning.

When he gets home, Nye stays up to have breakfast with Adrian and Amanda. After they have left for school, he goes to bed. He sleeps until about 3.30 in the afternoon and gets up just before the children get home.

As soon as Nye arrives at the pit head, he changes
into his work clothes, his pit helmet and his steel-
capped safety boots. He keeps them in a locker.
Then he goes to the lamp room to collect his head
lamp.

Nye goes to the pit shaft and waits for the *cage* to
take him underground. It's 300 metres to the
bottom of the pit.

A cross-section of a Welsh coal mine

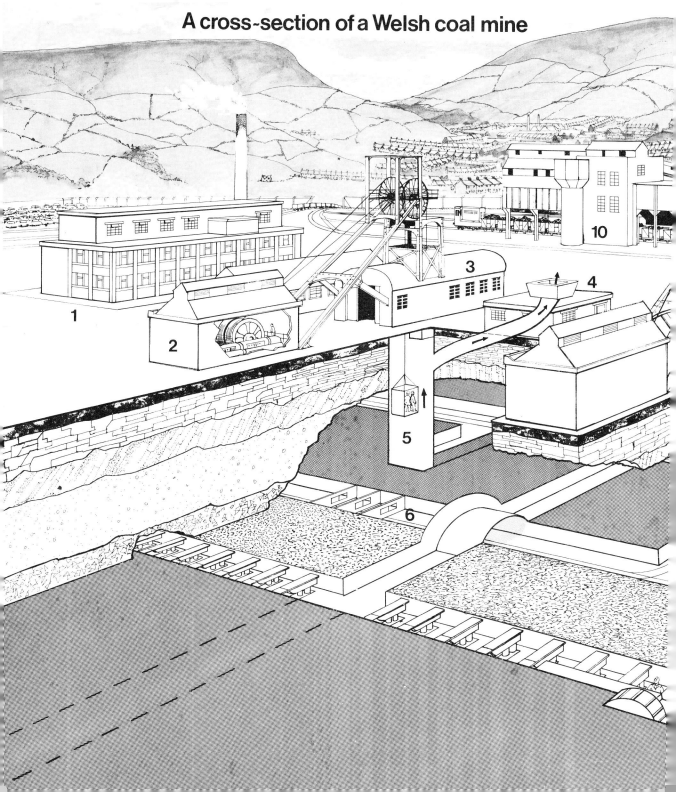

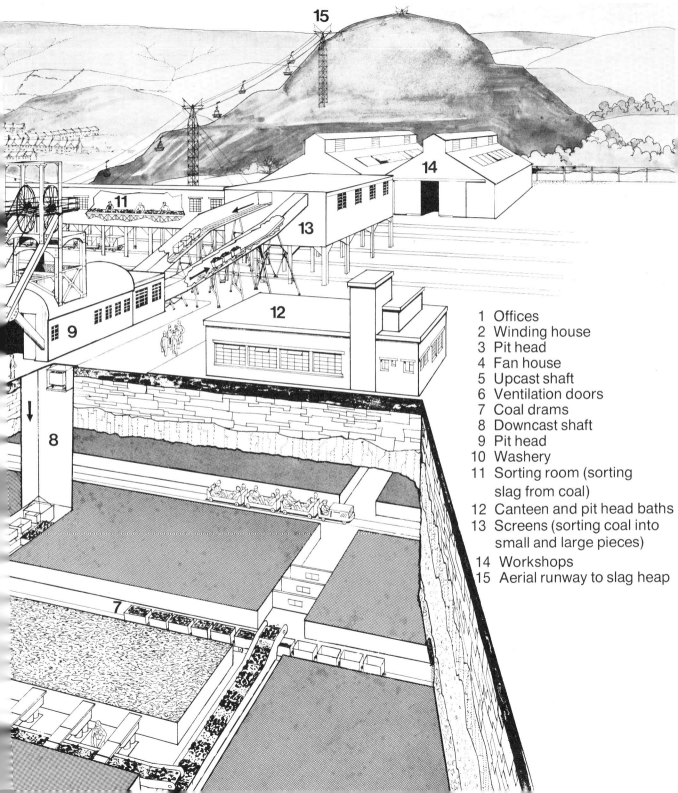

1 Offices
2 Winding house
3 Pit head
4 Fan house
5 Upcast shaft
6 Ventilation doors
7 Coal drams
8 Downcast shaft
9 Pit head
10 Washery
11 Sorting room (sorting
    slag from coal)
12 Canteen and pit head baths
13 Screens (sorting coal into
    small and large pieces)
14 Workshops
15 Aerial runway to slag heap

Nye is the safety officer. One of his jobs is to check there are no gas leaks. He uses a special kind of lamp.

He also checks that the hydraulic props are in good order. These are used to hold up the roof. They can be adjusted to fit the gap between the floor and the roof.

Another job Nye does is to check that the *drams* are running smoothly. A dram is a wagon in which coal is transported from the coal face to the surface. A conveyor belt loads the coal into the dram.

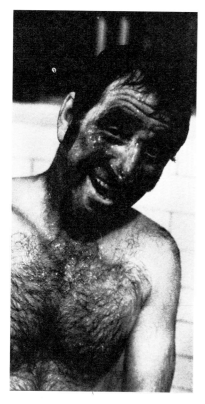

Nye is glad to get back above ground at the end of the shift. 'However long you work down a pit', he says, 'you never forget that you are always in danger.' He goes straight to the pit head baths where everyone is talking, laughing or singing. He spends a long time washing off the dirt. Then he changes into clean clothes, and goes to the canteen for a cup of tea.

Fifty years ago, there weren't any baths or canteens. The miners went home from work in dirty clothes. They washed in a tin bath in their own front room.

Mining is still a dirty and dangerous job. But conditions are better than they used to be. Miners today have a strong trade union, the NUM. In 1972 and 1974 the union voted to strike for more pay. Both strikes lasted for several months, and resulted in big pay increases for the miners. Since then most miners have been much better off.

Every year, all union members pay a sum of money to the NUM. Some of this money is used to build Miners' Welfare Clubs. People go to these clubs to meet their friends, and to have a drink or to dance. Every Saturday night, Nye and Anne go to the club in Abertillery. 'We meet most of our family there and have a good chat,' says Anne.

They usually see Uncle Dennis there. Like many people in Six Bells, Uncle Dennis keeps pigeons. He has a pigeon cot on his allotment. On Sundays, Adrian and Amanda often go to see the pigeons race.

Until quite recently, nearly everyone in the South Wales mining villages went to chapel on Sundays. Nowadays the chapels are half empty, and many have been put up for sale.

The number of choirs has dropped too, although South Wales has always been famous for its singing. Six Bells doesn't have a choir any longer, and people who want to join one have to go to Abertillery.

One Saturday every June, miners from all over Wales meet together in Cardiff. This day is known as Gala Day.

To open the Gala, there is a parade through the streets of the city. Miners and their families march behind banners saying which part of the country they come from. Everyone from Six Bells marches behind the Blaenau Gwent Joint Lodges banner.

They all march to tunes played by brass bands and jazz bands. After the parade, leaders of the miners' union give a speech to the crowd.

There is always lots to see and do. There are all sorts of competitions—for brass bands, jazz bands, folk dancing, rugby teams and football teams. The children compete in races and take turns at trampolining. Everywhere there are side shows and stalls, and plenty to eat and drink.

Gala day is the day when the miners come to town and show the people of Cardiff that there is something special about the mining villages.